Pluto

Frankie Sims

Presentation by *BookLeaf Publishing*

Web: www.bookleafpub.com

E-mail: info@bookleafpub.com

ISBN: 9789360940072

First edition 2024

*Dedicated to my younger self, who thought
she would never make it out of the pain.*

ACKNOWLEDGEMENT

This collection of poems could not have been possible without the support system I've grown along the way.

From starting my journey as an "aspiring" author at the age of 5, my family has been nothing but supportive. My mom specifically, said she would only read a finished work and never a work in progress. To my parents, brothers, and Grandma Sue, who always listened to my ideas even when they didn't make sense, thank you. You gave me the gift of writing and I'll use it forever, not always for good, but forever.

To my beautiful, wonderful, downright amazing partner, Kailani, thank you for always being my rubber duck. Every author needs someone to listen, troubleshoot, and love, and no matter the hour, you're always there. I love you and thank you for pushing me to write every single day.

To The Sanchez Family, some of my biggest fans, you guys are the most devoted, loyal bunch and I'm so happy to have you in my corner for this debut. I promise to sign your copies and not make it out to any cheesy nicknames I've given you over the past half-decade.

To Karen DeTomasi, Virginia Barr, and Julie Thompson, three educators who changed my life and how I viewed myself and my art. Without them, I would still be hiding my work in notebooks and crying before every PowerPoint presentation. You three have shaped my educational and creative journey more than you'll ever understand, and I hope I've made you proud.

To Valeria, Sigalu, Maxine, Kathryn, Haylee, Jazmine, and Daisy, the most dedicated friends I've ever had. They have all cheered for me at my worst (grammatically, I mean) and supported me endlessly at my best. They've read hours of my work and given me years of meaningful friendship along the way. I couldn't be happier to have had them with me throughout my journey as an author.

To Carolyn McMurray, Em Goodier, Leon Lynn, Em Thomas, Paris Cumba, Erin Norton, Sharmin A., and every beautiful soul who has participated in Word Tonic, THANK YOU. Word Tonic lit a writing fire under me that has never died and I am eternally grateful for the work it has provided me. Every word written, every day worked, I dedicate to the partnerships Word Tonic has brought to my life.

To my wonderful cover artist, Mila Klimkowicz, who made all my dreams come true. She worked with me day and night, through time-zones and time-crunches to make one of the most beautiful covers I've ever seen and I'm lucky enough for it to co-exist with my work. To have her art displayed on my bookshelf is an honor, and I could never thank her enough for the time, effort, and energy she put into this project. If you love the cover as much as I do and would like to see more of her work, visit her on Instagram @smoluglies.

Last but certainly not least, to River, Suki, Fish, Piper, Chowder, and Bella, thank you for always stepping on my keyboard and demanding pets right when I was getting to the good part. Your erasure and stomping of my work is an honor, and your wholesomeness made sitting at a desk for hours that much easier.

To everyone I mentioned and those I didn't get a chance to, thank you. I hope you'll love "Pluto" as much as I loved writing it.

PREFACE

Publishing "Pluto" was a no-brainer for me. I've waited years to gain my voice, to gain the courage, and to gain a laptop that could withstand my writing schedule, and I finally have it all. When I began writing, it was on blank pieces of printer paper around 5 years old, which I would write (and illustrate) on and try to gift to the member of my family I thought would appreciate it most. By the time I got into middle school, it was clear my love for writing wasn't going anywhere. I wrote dozens of online novels (that's what we'll call them) on websites like Wattpad, Movellas, and AO3. The community I built during that time was so wildly supportive, I was writing and people were READING, I was on top of the world. I loved every second of it. Once I graduated high school, I phased out of writing so much, it seemed like becoming an adult had sucked all the creativity out of my brain and told me NEWS FLASH: you can't write for a living. I had scraped by in Journalism during high school and knew I didn't want to work for KCRA3 or the Turlock Journal, so that wasn't an option I wanted to explore anymore. I took a long break from writing, it was painful, it felt like words were spilling out when I didn't want them and hiding from me when I needed them. In January 2024, I joined Word Tonic, a community of Gen-Z creative and copywriters that sparked a new love for writing I had been missing for half a decade. They inspired me to fill my social media feeds with other people who inspire me, not people who make me question my life choices.

So here we are, the stories you're about to read are those inspired but my lifetimes of grief, heartbreak, love, and joy. I hope that verbalizing my life experiences can bring comfort to others. To everyone who made this possible, thank you.

Frankie Sims

Pluto

I float in the dark
Sometimes aware of my surroundings
Big Bangs shaping craters around me
Black holes surround me
Siphoning my energy away

Who will remember me?

I was once the smallest
So small I seized to exist
Many thought of me this small to begin with
Someone forgettable
Someone who lacked something special

I fought for so long
Fought to be important
Yearned to be remembered
Cried to everyone above me
Screamed as I was crushed

I fear the world still turns without me
The sun still beams and thrives
The moon still finds purpose to rise

Venus still finds love

Mars forever befriends science
Jupiter will call the shots
Saturn and her rings still shine
Uranus tilts its head at every question
Neptune remains invisible to naked eyes

Somehow all more special than I
All more deserving of life

Maybe I have never been deserving of life

Bird of the River

Your home is a bird
A flightless bird of decades long gone
It perches
It watches
It remembers everything you may have forgotten

Standing guard of the basement you fear
It watches and waits
Scares off any intruders
It's a scarecrow of a house
Deceitfully quiet

Silent until the memories strike

The bird disappears at times
It packs up memories
Goes on vacation
Leaves you alone
Out on a thin branch
Broken and vulnerable without protection

Rivers call to the bird
Begging to be refilled
The bird brings suitcases of tears
Mixes them into the current

Adds ashes like flour

You rise every day
Without purpose
Without companion
Your bird returns happily
It's nest beside your bed

It pecks at your front door
Never loud enough for you to hear
It sneaks in through the chimney
No gifts to bring
Just sorrow weighing down its wings

Never questioned of pain
Scarcely offered stitches to it's wounds
Always assumed to be alive
Alive with the memory of the dead
The voices of those without

Laughing to match yours
Crying to catch your tears
Flightless to stay with you
Weighed down by choice
For gaining its wings would cause you pain

Leaving you would mean your name etched into
stone
The bird of the river would be without a home

35.4428 N, 120.8921 W

I feel closer to you
It's impossible to explain
You aren't buried there
You weren't married there

The streets boil over with memories
None of them belong to me
None of them can belong to you
You aren't here to tell me about them
You never had the chance to be

The sand sneaks into my shoes
Walking becomes a battle
Not with myself, but with you
Your spirit feels heavier near the water
It calls to me
I could drown in it

The gas station on the corner cries
Maybe it knows you died
Did your truck ever stop there?
It embraces me like an old friend
It sees my pain
It knows your face

Do you see your name on the pier?
It fades more every day
Your memory fades more as years pass
I hope we can all be together when it finally
disappears

You know where it hurts the most
The land that screams and goes hoarse
Begging for attention
Crying for a story
The story has always been you

I imagine your smile
The dreams you only had for a while
I start to believe
They died with you

But one day I'll make it a home
Build it from the ground up
Full of you, full of her
We wouldn't be here
If you hadn't been there

I'll have a stone
Place it beautifully in the garden
Your name forced onto it
Surrounded in life where you lack it

You should be here

Maybe someday you will be
Some day you will be home

I'll wait for you
Anytime you feel far
The Pacific is near
I'll drown in it one day
Fill it with tears
Leave a trail for you to follow

Some day, we'll be together.
Not again, but forever.

My Beautiful

Electric blue
Was it your eyes or the sky?
The room was a blue hue
Your eyes were due blue

 All I see is fog
The last sunrise of all
The sky was no longer blue
You were no longer you

Oh, what I would do
One more light
One more life
Your nine were never enough

The room is blue
Blue without you
Tears are falling
Not from the sky

The sky is dark
The light of stars is never enough
Your time was never enough

I hope your eyes are blue

Blue and full of life
Full of time.

Oh, what I would do
One more moment with you.

For our time could never be enough

You visit out of the blue
Stars light your way
If not stars, bright marigolds
A sunrise bright hue

The fog in my heart clears when you're near

But I turn blue when night falls once more
I picture the last night of all
You and I
Side by side
Your last breath quiet
My world went silent

Oh, what I would do for one more life

One more life with you.

For what we had, was never enough.

Water of Life

Burning
It travels my throat
Through my chest, it kills the pain
Settles into my stomach to poison me
Makes friends with my insides

They miss it as soon as it leaves
Send more through me
Keep the percentage growing
Let my insides sink or drown
I try to keep it down

Bring another round my way
Another shot won't hurt
My insides are scorched
My throat doesn't make a sound
I feel it fill me with life

Life to live another day
To win another fight
Trade one weapon for another
But my mouth is dry now
The bottle is empty

The crossroads stare into me

Do I follow a path well-paved
Or fight to swim against the current
To drag myself back home
Even when the floor calls to me
I don't know how I'm alive

I'll sleep tonight
Forget the burn in my throat
Avoid the spice in my chest
But tomorrow will be the same
The mirror behind the bar has no shame

Empty

What makes a bet worth losing your family?
Shining lights
Bright machines
Money flowing like water

Is fun worth losing your home?
One hour at a time
One drink at a time
Three hundred dollars at a time

Generations of pain
Generations of loss
Were the games you played worth it?

You'll lose your life to the addiction

Rabbit's Foot

Part of my heart was left on the 99
I saw it get ripped out of my chest
Torn in half
Thrown out the driver's side window

Highway 99 is an ocean now
Not from the fault
From the tears we cried
Spilling out the back window
 A waterfall into your truck bed

The 99-degree heat feels like lava
The windows are melting
The sun gives us no mercy
No sympathy in our worst hour

Your truck is a '99
The air suffocates us
The music fills the space
Where your words belong

I'm 99% sure this is the end
The end of my life as I know it
The end of our family
The end of normalcy

It was 99 minutes home in traffic
Every one of them worse than the last
The closer we got to home
The farther I was from you

I don't think you ever recovered
I don't think your heart rate ever dropped
Parts of us both were left there
Blowing somewhere in the wind
Out on Highway 99

When you turn 99 someday
You'll remember the songs we played
The rabbit's foot kept us safe that day
You kept your promise, all along

Man Made From Earth

Is a man made of Earth
When he is made of evil?
Can a man be born from the trees
And yet deadly as poison?

Can Mother Nature return him
Rebuild him whole
Throw out the bad roots
Sew him a soul

He's been rotting since birth
His leaves are all gone
No one dares to stick by him
It's impossible to keep him alive

He acts like the giving tree
But only feeds poisoned fruit
Nothing is accidental
Nothing is ever free

Can a man made from earth
Charge for his goods?
He may let you live
But he'll strip you of your worth

He disguises as an angel
Everyone can still see him coming
His name is a symbol
His eyes are a warning

It is impossible to trust
The man made from earth
As he is never changing
Not since his birth

Main St.

On Main St, there's a gas station
My nightmares live there

When I see it, my soul fills with gasoline
My lungs become flammable

He'll never know the pain
The part of me rotting in the alleyway
Left for dead

The whole store is up in flames in my head
It's a reminder of Hell
A grave to the ghost of who I once was

Main St isn't a road to me anymore
It's my resting place full of pain

Hidden

A game of hide and seek
Turned lifetime long

Closets are for clothes
They hide baggage, not bodies
Shield Christmas presents from young eyes

Where did she go?

A young girl hid there,
She was found changed.

She'll spend her whole life hiding now, don't
bother trying to find her.

I · XII · MMXVI

The hallway was dark
My thoughts were darker
My wrists were so torn
I didn't need to see them to feel the burn
To feel the vomit pooling at my throat

Walking out was a mistake
The cold air choked me
It didn't intend on letting me live
But I couldn't walk fast enough
Anxiety made my legs go numb
Frostbite had no work left to do

Where I would go?
How much longer would I survive?
How much longer could I fight?

There wasn't any room left on my wrists.
I would have to move on.
Move on to a better place
Somewhere no one would hurt me
Not even myself.

Every car whirring by was a nightmare
The fog couldn't hide me for long

I couldn't hide from my death sentence much
longer
Today might be my execution.

There was no one around to help
No one to call if I went missing
Nowhere to go but home

"Where are you? We need to talk."

If only the sidewalk ended here.

One foot in front of the other
One nightmare minute at a time

I think I'm running now
I can't breathe
My legs won't slow down
My lungs won't catch up
My eyes won't dry.

Was it the pain in my scars running through my
veins? Was it the adrenaline pushing my body
forward?

It was like flipping a coin, life or death. I was
hoping for death.

Red flags had all been missed, only a coroner
tag could send the message. My sloppy,
tear-smeared handwriting couldn't convey the
pain. Nothing could come close to explaining it.

I'm on the floor now.
I think I'm breathing,
I can't be sure.

Nothing is sure anymore. Tomorrow is unsure.
I'm unsure.

Why, me? Why, anyone?

I dream of death row, daydream of solitary
confinement. Nowhere else is safe, no one can
be trusted to save me.

I'm thirteen and alone.

If I make it to July, I'll be fourteen.

If I make it to next year, I'll be a Freshman in
high school.

If I make it to 2020, I'll finally be free.

I won't hold my breath.

Golden Years

I miss you
Not you now, but you a lifetime ago
You when you cared
You when you liked to see me
You when you weren't sharp to the touch

You now is like a serrated blade
I feel everything
Every ridge, every tear
I think you stabbed me when I was born
I don't think I've ever lived without this wound
The blade lives inside me now
Still cutting
Still tearing
But you don't see the damage you've caused

There was a time
You could only hurt me physically
Never with lasting injuries
That time ended a lifetime ago
It ended when I learned to stand up for myself
When I learned to fight back

You didn't like that I fought back
You didn't approve of me growing into my voice

Everyone tried to warn me

"Take it to the grave," you said
As if you'd be the one to put me there
Like I wasn't losing blood by the second
My serrated blade held me closer
I could feel it cutting deeper

I don't blame you for hurting
But sometimes I hate you for not understanding
This could've brought us closer
Could've mended our generational pain
But you decided you didn't want that
All you wanted was to watch me bleed

I remember all the times you wouldn't speak to
me
I begged you to say anything at all
Even if all you said was that you hated me
I wanted to fight for you
I wanted to help you heal

The blade is still stuck in me
I think I'll live with it forever
It takes your place somehow
Fills the hole you left in my story
My story you wish had ended

I still watch in silence

Watch you pour gasoline on our family tree
Stare into me while you strike a match
Tell everyone I threw it into the fire

Maybe someday I'll burn it
Not the tree, but the bridge between us
I'll watch it turn to ash
While you scream and cry from the other side
No apology in sight
No empty words left to hurt me
I'll leave you behind
I'll stitch up my wound

The scar will stay behind
It'll remind me of me, not of you
Maybe I don't miss you anymore

Under the Oak Tree

If I die by a gun
Don't pretend you weren't on the enemy side
Don't pretend you weren't a sponsor
Don't pretend you cared

If I die by a gun
Don't change your mind
Don't pretend to be woke
Don't be mad at anyone but yourself

If I die by a gun
Think of all the others before me
Think of the ones we tried to prevent
Think of the ones you never believed

When I die by a gun
Don't say I was right
Admit you were wrong
Tell the world you never listened
Drown in your embarrassment
Watch the world erupt
Not in war, but in thoughts and prayers

Don't lie to yourself
Don't pretend you didn't force it into my hand

Don't pretend you didn't make them pull the
trigger
Don't blame it on anyone but yourself
Your selfishness
Your lack of care for human life
Your lack of care for anything besides what's
"right"

All I ask is that you remember me.

Spread my ashes around the Oak tree, watch me
grow into something you're proud of. Something
you can't kill. Something you can't vote for.

Maybe you'll cut me down to pen your next law.

When I die by a gun.

5AM

27

Alone in the sun
The sun rises to keep my company

Smoke clouds my vision
Keeps my lungs from seeing the cars pass by

The streets are quiet
The Willamette Bridge wakes as commuters fly

The world is asleep
It begins to feel like it may never wake up

I wish I could wake up
I don't want to be alone anymore
Alone in this nightmare

Vineyard

Mother Earth
Spitting out vineyards
Building life's wine through her body
Rooting her children into maturity

Beautiful they become
A destination
A journey to be enjoyed
A precious winery among the mountains

Mother loves her children
Always watching them grow
Always giving them the life they need
Shaping them into the finest wine money can
buy

All she ever wanted was her children
Her children to be loved
To be adored
To be alive

To be a child of our mother is to know love
To understand the connection from one vine to
another
The intertwining of generational pain

Mixed with sweet healing

My mother is a beautiful vineyard
A family cared for
A lifetime of experience
A glass of wine to hold you close

Freedom

To be yours is to never be my own
Wanted by mother, hated by self
Tied to the past
Forced to the ground

To be her is to be a stranger
Someone unfamiliar
A ghost of the pain I've left
A name in an obituary unwritten

To stay with her is to be an outsider
Always left out
Never not alone
Stuck in the dark
No light to lead the way

My freedom brings a clean slate
A reborn mind
Free space for new memories
Pre-dug graves for the old to crawl into
My mind is a field of flowers

Finally growing
I feel the sun on my skin
The skin I always hid under sleeves

The light charges life into me
Shines a future into my mind

To be free is to be me
Without strings
Without pain attached

To be wanted by nobody but myself, as I am all
that I need.

Ascend

Wind in my ears
Life in my eyes
If I think hard enough,
I might start to fly

Ascend beyond who I've become
Above the sky
Past the stars

All I feel is power
The never-ending force of life running through
my veins

For once, I'm unstoppable
The Moon reaches out to me
Carries me out from our sunroof
Cradles me into the darkness
Teaches me the journey of life

The stars are my family
All they do is shine for me
They will always guide me

Heavenly Sea

Knowing a light
For once a sign that I'm alive
Not that I'm dying
I see it come towards me
It's warmth overcomes me
Unlike anything I've felt ever before

Angelically, it melts my pieces back together
Effortlessly, without complaint
Welding my broken heart
Embracing me like we've met before
Like it's known me forever
As if it's loved me my whole life

It feels familiar, but foreign in every way
It shines heavenly
Beams into my skin
It warms my frozen lungs
Breathes life into me
A life I didn't know I was missing
A love I didn't recognize

Light chooses to stay with me
She says I clear the skies
I help her shine brighter than ever before

She'll never know how bright she is
She's heavenly

And when it rains
Or even when it snows
She lights up so bright
I could never be cold
She radiates an infinite warmth
A life-force no one can stop or slow down

Nothing could compare
Even when she's angry
Even when she's happy
Her light never dims
It fills the sky through the night and through the
day
The sun and the moon could seize to exist with
her here

I love this light.
It's beauty follows me through life
Let me cry on her shoulder
Warms my soul when the Earth turns me cold
When I hide in the darkness

The light asks me one day if she can stay forever
As if she even had to ask
I don't think I could live without her
She's a part of me now

She's built into my heart
Stitched into every vein
Holding my hand through every cloud
Every thunderstorm
She never dims.

Our love will never dim.

As long as the sun will rise and the night will
fall.

She will catch every darkness that falls on me
and every tear that drops into her heavenly sea.

High House of Learning

The busy streets could never bother me, for I am home.

My home is here
The high house of learning

I've learned to feel, to see, to hear the world around me

The air flows in the windows like an old friend
Stray cats stare with adoration
Sirens blare at the quietest hour

But I am home

My safety, my solitude

My house of learning

Learning to live and learning to love

Filled with love
Light beaming through the windows
Love spilling from the kitchen

My beautiful home, I longed for you so long.

Carried with me, you always will be. My home
of lessons learned.

Solar System

How can a solar system co-exist for so long
Only to become foreign to itself
To break apart into one million pieces
Seize to fit together
Like pieces from different puzzles

Maybe they never did fit
I wouldn't have realized
"In every universe"
I see you in every universe

You're every store at the mall
Every shirt I know you'd buy
Every empty space, now filled with old
memories
Never new ones

You're every faded Polaroid picture
Every stupid Snapchat memory
Every plan we made for futures changed
How did we end up strangers?

You sound like every song
Every live-music memory
If I close my eyes

I can take myself there again

You've become every dream
Every nightmare
I can't decide which is worse

You live in every story told
Most tears shed
And pictures I can't bear to look at
Most get shredded
Then filled with regret

We've become enemies somehow
Every message goes unsent
Every effort unreturned
I don't blame you
I just don't always understand
But I don't think I need to
I think it would break me worse

I'll always remember you
I'll always keep the memories alive
I can't imagine a day they won't feel fresh
A day where it wasn't yesterday I saw you for
the last time
And didn't realize you planned on never coming
back

I would've hugged you tighter

I wouldn't have let you leave
I would've told you more
I could have changed your mind

But all you did was leave
No "I'm sorry"
No warning
No new memories to leave me with
Just like that
You were gone

You were all gone.

Now I cry
I wake up gasping for air
The empty space you left chokes me

I don't like remembering you this way
You should be acknowledged
Not forgotten
Not labeled "Painful, do not open"
Not a figment of my imagination when I feel
like hurting

But I know you're happier
I'm happier
It's a hard pill to swallow sometimes
To know the universe never meant to have us
together forever

I would've slowed down the solar system
Made Earth spin slower
Burned in the scorching sun
Just to be by your side
I would have laid with you longer
Staring at our fate in the stars
Crying for hours
Blaming nothing but ourselves

But I'd like to think you're better now
All the planets feel at ease
Everything is aligned
The universe put us where we belong

After all, Pluto only exists if you want it to.

For you, I am Pluto.

Lost in the darkness, lost in space.

I will only allow myself to exist for those who
choose to remember me.

I don't think you'll ever be sober enough to
remember me.

www.ingramcontent.com/pod-product-compliance
Lightning Source LLC
La Vergne TN
LVHW050944200726
843508LV00011B/2442